50 LESSONS
IN 50 YEARS

Dedicated to my brother, my mentor,
my business partner, my kindred spirit –
Jack Kinder, Jr.

GARRY KINDER

50 LESSONS IN 50 YEARS

Printed in the United States of America
ISBN: 0-9788137-1-5

Credits
Design, art direction, and production   Melissa Monogue, Back Porch Creative, Plano, TX
info@BackPorchCreative.com

Dedicated
to
Jack Kinder, Jr.

Mentor – Counselor – Brother

Jack and Garry crossing the finish line at the 2005 Tyler Cup
three months before Jack had a stroke.
This was the finish for a two-mile run.

Life is not finished. There is still much to be done in Jack's honor.

ACKNOWLEDGEMENTS

This book has truly been a labor of love. My brother, Jack, and his wife, Mary Sue, have always been an inspiration to me. They have been close friends. Jack has been a mentor, a counselor and a brother. Thanks to them for their inspiration and guidance over the years.

Thanks to my wife, Janet, for her patience. She has been very helpful in listening to me talk about all these principles and share my thoughts as they relate to family matters. Janet was very close to my mother and father. Because of this, she could see where many of these lessons had initially been learned.

Thanks to my children, grandchildren and sons-in-law for their constant love and loyalty.

Thanks to Lu Ann Butler, who has worked for Kinder Brothers for 26 years. She is a faithful employee, but more importantly, she is a friend. Through her years at our company, she's witnessed many of these lessons in the making.

Thanks to Helen Hosier for writing the introduction. She is a gifted author who can take any situation and write about it fluently.

Thanks to the many friends, family members, teammates and professors who have helped me experience these great lessons of life.

To all of you in the financial services industry, we say thank you for everything you have done for us, our families and our business. We are proud to be in this great business.

PREFACE

On January 31, 2006, my brother, Jack, suffered a massive stroke. It was then I decided to put together *50 Lessons in 50 Years* – 50 things that I've learned in 50 years. Twenty-one of these lessons I learned before I ever entered the life insurance business.

At age 20, I entered the life insurance business as a junior in college. I'm one of those rare people who came out of college knowing full well I was going into the life insurance business. Today, it's the financial services industry; then, it was the life insurance business. I followed my brother, Jack, into a sales career with Equitable Life of New York, known today as AXA.

Many of you reading this book have known us for a long time – 50-plus years. Many of you will be hearing of the Kinder brothers for the first time. We've been in the financial services industry for more than 50 years. Since 1976, through our consulting firm, The KBI Group, we've enjoyed teaching and mentoring tens of thousands of agents and managers in hundreds of companies, domestically and internationally. I want to share these lessons with you and all who will enter this great business.

Some of these lessons we've learned recently – some many, many years ago. All are relevant for today and long into the future. I trust and I pray these 50 lessons will help you in your professional and personal life.

Garry D. Kinder

Portrait by friend, Dennis McClain
Photo by friend, Rob Hinds

TWO BROTHERS
FROM THE LAND OF THE FREE
AND THE HOME OF THE BRAVE

By Helen Kooiman Hosier

It made my day when I was asked to write an introduction about these two giants in the financial services industry – the Kinder brothers – Jack and Garry. I have written many stories of peoples' lives, and the stories of these two men has certainly captured my attention.

Jack and Garry Kinder come from a traditional, functional, Midwestern family. Their parents came through the Great Depression and never forgot those years. To their sons they passed on the valuable lessons learned through that experience. The years of World War II left an impression and also shaped their thinking. This is truly the land of the free and the home of the brave.

Jack and Garry Kinder: From Pekin, Illinois, to Equitable to KBI
Through the example of their parents, Jack and Garry were taught the value of hard work and the need for discipline to become loyal, trustworthy and successful individuals. Neither of their parents, nor they themselves in those growing-up years, would have attached the word *integrity* to what was taking place, but the value of adhering to that which is honest and morally sound was certainly occurring. The road to success and leadership for them was paved with application of principles learned in the home and a Midwest community that encouraged old-fashioned integrity.

You hold in your hands a valuable book. Books don't just miraculously happen, books develop because someone has something to share, and they've done more than dream about being successful. Following the dreaming, there has been constancy and consistency of effort in pursuit of the lessons that this book expounds. Those lessons are extensive and ever-growing. Indeed, they are still on the journey.

Boyhood Years

Imagine two boys growing up in the same household; one is five years older than the other. Garry Kinder says of his brother, "Jack and I have been together from the very beginning. In fact, he knew me before anybody else!" Garry would make the journey into the world with a brother near at hand. The day would come when Jack would take that little fellow by the hand and introduce him to that big, wide world. Together they would do the fun things that brothers do. They would disagree about things now and then, as siblings are apt to do, but together they would experience the discipline and teachings of their mother and father. They would play and pray; learn and grow.

Jack preceded his brother into the school years. There were some definite advantages to having a brother who had been there, done that. Garry benefited from the wisdom that was accruing in his big brother, and Jack was a good teacher, even as a child. The junior high years saw Jack and Garry being influenced by their grandfather to play the trombone. "Grandpa was a great trombonist and wanted us to play, but we wanted to be athletes," Garry remembers.

Pekin High School

Each attended Pekin Community High School where they were members of the National Honor Society and pursued their athletic dreams. They each participated in three sports – baseball, basketball and football. Jack was All-State in basketball and Garry was All-State in baseball. Both were captains of their football, basketball and baseball teams. Both were quarterbacks and point guards. Jack was the shortstop for the baseball team; Garry was the catcher.

They worked hard at athletics and they excelled. They learned about sportsmanship, rules and fair play – needful disciplines they would carry with them forever.

Each of them benefited from their parent's wisdom and instruction. Wise sayings were intertwined in the daily conversation of this mother and father, falling on listening ears and into hearing hearts. They were good listeners – listening to learn – developing empathy and respect for the opinions of others.

Parental Principles

The work ethic was clearly defined by the example of their father. "Our dad taught us to work, taught us discipline, and taught us to tithe 10 percent and to save 10 percent." That meant that God was to receive 10 percent. These parental principles were enforced, but the sons learned the lessons that came from giving with a cheerful heart to the German/Dutch church they attended as a family. "Rain, sleet or snow, we were in church. No exceptions were allowed," they recall. The boys also saw their own savings grow. Each son never deviated from what they were taught as they continued their journey from boyhood to young adulthood to maturity.

The brothers saw that many of life's greatest satisfactions would come, not from leisure, but from work well done, wholeheartedly. Daily goal setting and work-habit strengtheners were built into their thinking even as young boys.

Their German background also brought perseverance into their lives. For example, at an early age Garry seriously injured his arm and the doctor said that he might end up having a stiff arm. Upon hearing this, Mrs. Kinder said to the doctor, "Don't you ever talk like that in front of my son again. He will not have a stiff arm. I'll see to it that he doesn't." She did just that by forcing Garry to exercise and stretch the arm twice a day for three months to prevent it from getting stiff. Garry was introduced to pain and what can happen when one doesn't give up and give in to that which is difficult and painful. Today, he doesn't have a stiff arm.

Early Work Experiences

This strong work ethic was consistently ingrained in them from a father who worked for 50 years at Keystone Steel and Wire. "He began there when he was 15 and worked there until he was 65. To our knowledge, he never missed a day of work for any reason." Work experiences for each of them began at an early age. Jack was 10 when he had his first paying job as caddie at Pekin Country Club. "My first customer, Mr. Velde, encouraged me. 'You're a clean-cut boy and well mannered. You'll be an A-Class caddie one of these days.' He gave me $1, which was the going rate for C-Class caddies, and a generous 25-cent tip. From that day to this day, I've had a job and money in my pocket."

Garry's experiences show a pattern of moving from one job into another that was better paying and offered him new and valuable learning experiences. Garry and Jack worked hard at jobs during high school and college.

Og Mandino wrote [that] "*You cannot command success – you can only deserve it. You are more than a human being; you are a human becoming.*" The Kinder brothers were becoming as they moved into college and higher learning that propelled them ever forward.

Illinois Wesleyan University

The Kinder brothers went to Illinois Wesleyan University. Jack became an outstanding college basketball player. Garry was the quarterback on the first undefeated team at the university; however, a hand injury cut Garry's athletic career short. Jack had set his sights on being a college coach. "I thought colleges would be knocking my door down to get me as a coach. When they didn't, I left after three years of high school coaching in Chicago. If I could have gotten a college coaching job, I'd still be coaching." But this was not the direction his life should go, and he is quick to admit that God had other plans for him. He had majored in education and minored in business. Business beckoned.

Garry majored in business with a minor in education. Both men graduated with honors from Illinois Wesleyan University. They have served as co-chairmen of the Alumni Association, and Garry still serves on the Board of Trustees.

Equitable Life

Jack had found a niche that fit him comfortably in the insurance business and he became licensed at Equitable Life, which is now known as AXA, one of the largest insurance companies in the world. He was recruited into the insurance business by Fred G. Holderman, the first man inducted into the General Agents and Managers Association (GAMA) Hall of Fame.

Jack recruited Garry while he was still a junior in college. Garry was 20. They had discovered something that motivated them; they became committed to excellence, and their enthusiasm and persistence paid off. Selling seemed to be in their blood. As insurance agents, they delivered ideas and services to consumers through the products they had to offer. Needs were being met; clients were satisfied.

Albert Einstein said to try not to become a man of success, but rather try to become a man of value. Jack and Garry Kinder were becoming men of value. Self-discipline, imagination and staying power fueled their efforts as they became peak performers. Not only had they become high achievers, they were men of integrity.

Moving up through the ranks saw the brothers earning superior selling credentials and they became managers. Both earned the Chartered Life Underwriter (CLU) designation in 1962. They have been members of the National Association of Insurance and Financial Advisors (NAIFA) for more than 50 years. They both have their Certified Senior Advisor (CSA) and Registered Financial Consultant (RFC) designations. They have both been Equitable's Young Manager of the Year. They were managing directors of the Purdue Management Institute for 30 years.

Million Dollar Round Table (MDRT)
They qualified for the Million Dollar Round Table (MDRT) at young ages, as well as being qualifying members in 2001 and 2003. They have conducted workshops at the MDRT conventions in Orlando and Toronto.

In 1976, Jack and Garry formed Kinder Brothers International. Building in-depth training programs for more than 300 companies, domestically and internationally, has kept the brothers on their toes.

Strong Faith
Both men have been active in civic affairs. They have taught Bible studies every Sunday and are active members of the First Baptist Church in Dallas. Jack was the founder of the IMPACT Group, a non-denominational Bible study in Dallas. Garry has taught the Bent Tree Bible Study for more than 26 years. He was a founder of the Bent Tree Counseling Center and the Roaring Lambs Foundation.

The strong faith of the two brothers has been at the apex of everything they have done. Their belief in God and His precepts has been, and is, what guides their thinking and decision-making. They subscribe to the idea that "*Life is God's gift to us, what we do with it is our gift to God.*" Strength, vitality and optimism come from spiritual harmony, according to one of their books.

Family Life

Jack and his wife, Mary Sue, have one married daughter, Jayne Ann. Jayne and her husband, Craig, have three children, all of whom are outstanding athletes. Jack is proud of the fact that his two grandsons are Eagle Scouts. Today, Chase is the starting quarterback at Rice University.

Garry was married to Barbara for 34 years before she was tragically killed in October 1990. He has since married Janet, who lost her husband to cancer in 1985. They have four children and six grandchildren. Garry's son-in-law, David Smith, is active at Kinder Brothers heading up corporate sales. His other son-in-law, Curt Ladd, is a 23-year member of the MDRT, having made Top of the Table three years and Court of the Table twice.

January 31, 2006

On January 31, 2006, Jack Kinder, the elder of the two brothers, suffered a massive stroke. There was nothing unusual about the morning at all in Rock Island, Illinois. As was his custom, Jack rose early and headed to the exercise facility at his hotel before heading off to conduct a management seminar. This was to be one of four such meetings in this typical week. After exercising, Jack became disoriented but was able to make his way to the front desk to get help.

Garry was just about to board a plane heading to Boston for a meeting when he received the call that his brother, Jack, had suffered a massive stroke. In one short, monumental moment, their lives and business were forever changed.

After some recovery time in the hospital, Jack was able to move on to physical and speech therapy. His approach to the rehabilitation process is as you would imagine – expecting and getting the best from himself and others.

The Kinder brothers have spent their lives passionately investing in others. Jack Kinder has the marvelous gifts of vision and getting others to follow and be at their best. He loves the written word. Throughout his career, Jack has used the written word to communicate powerful and much-needed lessons and information. Jack is a master communicator.

This is what inspired Garry Kinder to share these 50 lessons and dedicate this book to the great Jack Kinder – his brother, his business partner, his counselor, his friend.

Reprinted with permission of the publisher from *Building the Master Agency*, by Jack and Garry Kinder, with Val Ivanov, Copyright 2002, The National Underwriter Company.

CONTENTS

DEDICATION   *i*

ACKNOWLEDGEMENTS   *ii*

PREFACE   *iii*

TWO BROTHERS FROM THE LAND OF THE FREE
AND THE HOME OF THE BRAVE   *iv*
   (by Helen Kooiman Hosier)

WHAT I LEARNED FROM MY DAD   **1**
Lesson 1   Work hard, it cures almost all
             your problems   3
Lesson 2   Give 10% to the church   6
Lesson 3   Save 10% of everything you make   7

WHAT I LEARNED FROM MY MOM   **9**
Lesson 4   Show up at church every Sunday   11
Lesson 5   Be frugal; spend your money wisely   13
Lesson 6   Be pleasant, be nice to people   14
Lesson 7   Spend several hours a day reading   15

WHAT I LEARNED FROM MY BROTHER   **17**
Lesson 8   Systematize everything   18
Lesson 9   You play like you practice   20
Lesson 10   Keep your eye on the ball (pay attention)   21

WHAT I LEARNED FROM MY EARLY PASTORS   **23**
Lesson 11   Dr. Zimmerman taught me I could be
             a force for good or a force for evil   24
Lesson 12   Dr. Martin told me I could do more as
             a layman than as a pastor   25

WHAT I LEARNED FROM MY COACHES   27

Lesson 13   I learned more on the playing field than
I ever did in the classroom   28

Lesson 14   I learned teamwork   30

Lesson 15   I learned the most important word
in the English language: Discipline   31

WHAT I LEARNED FROM MY FRATERNITY BROTHERS   33

Lesson 16   I learned more from my fraternity
brothers than I did in the classroom   34

Lesson 17   I learned how to get along with all types of people   34

Lesson 18   I learned to sacrifice for the good of the cause   36

WHAT I LEARNED FROM MY LIFE INSURANCE PROFESSOR   37

Lesson 19   Be a student of the business   38

Lesson 20   Buy all the life insurance the company will issue   39

Lesson 21   Always buy permanent life insurance   40

Lesson 22   Make decisions on how they are going
to affect you 15 years from today   41

WHAT I LEARNED FROM EARL NIGHTINGALE   43

Lesson 23   Ideas and concepts are what change
people's lives   44

Lesson 24   Read one good book every month on
how to live and how to work   46

Lesson 25   Good stuff in, good stuff out; bad
stuff in, bad stuff out   47

WHAT I LEARNED FROM THE FINANCIAL SERVICES INDUSTRY   49

Lesson 26   Winners keep on winning; losers keep on losing   50

Lesson 27   Nothing is as constant as change   51

Lesson 28   Change is inevitable; growth is optional   53

Lesson 29   Memorize the scripts; ad libs are for amateurs   53

Lesson 30   Successful people form habits of doing
things failing people don't do   56

Lesson 31   Take care of your clients; eventually your
clients will take care of you   58

MORE LESSONS FROM THE FINANCIAL SERVICES INDUSTRY 61

Lesson 32	It's always better to pay too much than to pay too little	62
Lesson 33	Pay too much, you lose a little money; pay too little, you could lose everything	62
Lesson 34	When buying clothes, pay twice as much, buy half as many	63
Lesson 35	Spectacular achievements come from unspectacular preparation	64
Lesson 36	Think about the solution, not the problem	65
Lesson 37	Great performers do not wait for inspiration	66
Lesson 38	Show up on time, dressed, ready to play	67
Lesson 39	Make every occasion a great occasion	68
Lesson 40	Utilize the wise counsel of others	69

EVEN MORE LESSONS FROM THE FINANCIAL SERVICES INDUSTRY 71

Lesson 41	Never confuse activity with accomplishment	72
Lesson 42	Honest, intelligent effort is always rewarded	73
Lesson 43	Strategies won't work unless you do	75
Lesson 44	Professionals are at their best – regardless	75
Lesson 45	Don't expect perfection – expect excellence	76
Lesson 46	When people stop getting better, they cease to be good	77
Lesson 47	There's no second chance to make a good first impression	79
Lesson 48	Don't waste your time with those who waste your time	79

WHAT I LEARNED FROM DR. W.A. CRISWELL 81

Lesson 49	Life is short, life is fragile	82
Lesson 50	Love never divides, it always multiplies	85

THE BEST IS YET TO BE! 87

I'D RATHER SEE A SERMON 88

WHAT I LEARNED FROM
MY DAD

LESSON 1
WORK HARD, IT CURES ALMOST ALL YOUR PROBLEMS

My dad would say to my brother, Jack, and me, "Work hard, it will cure almost all your problems. Be a hard worker. Be known around town as a person who's a hard worker. People like to do business with hard workers. They like to do business with people who are serious about their business."

My dad never got out of the third grade. At least that's what he told Jack and me. We discussed it many times and decided we weren't so sure he ever got into the third grade.

My dad grew up in an era when honesty, hard work, commitment and loyalty reigned supreme. He never knew his dad. His mother was blind, but not surprisingly, a strong person. She died when Jack and I were young.

Dad had to go to work at a young age. Of course, that was not uncommon back then. At age 15, he went to work for Keystone Steel and Wire in Peoria, Illinois. He worked there 50 years and retired at age 65. Fifty years at one place – and most of those years he walked the nine miles to work.

As I look back, I can never, ever remember my dad being sick. I know he had to be sick sometime. He was never seriously sick, never in the hospital. But he had to wake up some days and not be feeling too well! In all those years, I don't ever remember him missing a day of work. In those days, you just didn't miss work. If you had the flu, you worked … runny nose, you worked. He'd get up every morning and go to work. In the evenings, he'd come back to the house and go to work at home. He would work on the furnace, mow the lawn or plant a garden. Whatever needed tending to, Dad did it. He was a good role model for Jack and me.

He also taught us how to make money. And there is a difference between just working hard and making money.

It would snow a lot in Illinois. He'd rattle us out of bed at 6 a.m. and say, "It's snowing out there. You need to get out and shovel the walks. When you finish with our driveway, you go up and down the streets and knock on doors, because people will want their walks shoveled. They'll pay you a little something for it." And they would – they would pay us $1.

In the summer, we mowed lawns and raked leaves. When we were in college, he put us to work at Keystone Steel and Wire in the steel mill. I know why he did it. He wanted to teach us to stay in college or else we were going to end up in that steel mill. We didn't want to end up there. I couldn't wait until I graduated from college so I wouldn't have to go back to that kind of work.

I learned from my dad to get up and go to work; it will cure almost all your problems.

Hard work spotlights the character of people:
some turn up their sleeves,
some turn up their noses,
and some don't turn up at all.
– Sam Ewig

This is the house where many of these lessons were learned.

Grandma Kinder – totally blind.

LESSON 2
GIVE 10% TO THE CHURCH

My dad taught us to tithe – give 10% to the church. He said, "You take 10% of everything you make and give it to the church. Do you understand that biblical principle?"

We went to the kind of church where they would give you offering envelopes. Dad would give us our envelopes and these instructions: "Every time you make a dollar shoveling snow, you put 10% in this envelope. Every time your mother or I, or anybody, gives you any kind of money, you put 10% in this envelope. You give 10% to the church before you do anything else."

> *I've always operated on the principle that your first real*
> *dollar isn't the first dollar that you earn.*
> *Your first real dollar is the one that you give away.*
> – Michael Roux

Jack and Garry growing up, pictured with Mom and Dad.

LESSON 3

SAVE 10% OF EVERYTHING YOU MAKE

He taught us 10 and 10 – 10% to the church, 10% to the savings account.

At age five, I was about three feet tall – and I'm not exaggerating – I was just high enough to reach the counter at Hergets' Bank. Dad took me to that window and said, "This young boy here wants to open up a savings account." He said, "Now 10% of everything you make goes into this account."

We have taught this to our children and through them to our grandchildren. We have taught them that 10% of everything they receive goes to the church and 10% of everything they receive goes in a savings account.

By the time our children arrived at college age, those young people had enough money in their savings to use for spending money. Today, they are passing these lessons on to their kids – 10% to the church – 10% to your savings account.

When I give the grandkids a little cash for a birthday or on a holiday, I say to them, "Now where does the first 10% go?" "Church." "Now where does the second 10% go?" "Savings account."

We're teaching them the same philosophy that my dad taught me years ago.

It's not how much you make that counts, but how much money you keep. It's best to save first and spend last.

WHAT I LEARNED FROM MY MOM

LESSON 4
SHOW UP AT CHURCH EVERY SUNDAY

My brother and I were athletes. Jack was first team All-State in basketball and, for awhile, pursued a career in coaching.

At 16, it seemed like every time I played a baseball game there was a scout there watching. We had a semi-pro league in Peoria. Back in those days, they paid the pitcher and the catcher cash. Being a young catcher, I would make cash every time I would play a semi-pro game. This is completely illegal today, probably was back then, but nobody knew it. Sometimes on Sundays, I could catch as many as four games, but my mother said to me: "You are not catching any baseball games on Sunday until you are 16 years old. You are going to church every Sunday, no exceptions. I don't care how much they are paying you. You are not going to play any baseball games. You are going to church. Do you understand?" I would say, "Yeah, Mom, I do."

And what I didn't understand, my dad would help me understand – real fast! Dad had a way of communicating without many words. Do you know what a barrel stave is? Well, that's what they made barrels out of back in those days. They wrapped wire around them, then filled the barrel with nails or other materials. Keystone Steel and Wire would allow employees to take home any broken barrel staves. They were good for kindling wood. But my dad didn't use them for kindling wood; my dad used them to teach us a lesson. And he taught me a lot of lessons. He taught me far more lessons than he taught Jack, because I needed a little more "lesson learning" than Jack did.

He never did say to me – ever – "Now this is going to hurt me worse than it's going to hurt you." Dad would say, "Young man – this is gonna hurt!!"

One day Jack and I went out and surveyed the neighborhood. We decided it was a good day to redo our baseball field across the street – you know, a sandlot baseball field. Jack and I figured it needed a little help. It was raining, and we said, "Boy, this is ideal. Let's get some mud and we can spread it around the way we want it." So here we were in the rain and my mother is out there on the front porch hollering at us, "You boys get home – now! You wait 'til your dad gets home!!"

We came home all covered in mud. It was everywhere. When Dad got home, he took care of us both at once using those barrel staves, like you wouldn't believe.

So I knew I better show up at church. And I showed up at church 16 straight years. I never missed one Sunday of church in 16 years – never – not once for sickness, for rain, sleet, snow. I showed up at church.

Now, just showing up at church doesn't have a lot to do with becoming a good Christian; it really doesn't have anything to do with it. It just means I showed up at church. I will say this though, you can't show up at church and Sunday school for 16 years straight and sit there without learning something. If we would go on vacation, which was rare, we'd have to get a report from the visiting Sunday school class that we showed up there and take it back to our Sunday school class, because they gave you stars if you showed up 52 weeks. Well, I got all the stars and so did Jack.

I learned from my mother – show up at church!!

Always make the main thing the main thing.

Note on back of picture written by "Mom" Kinder:
*Jack - age 10, Garry - age 5. Notice Sunday school pin
on suit for perfect attendance at Sunday school.*

LESSON 5

BE FRUGAL; SPEND YOUR MONEY WISELY

My mother knew how to handle money. We were never in debt for anything, but we weren't making any money. My dad wasn't making much money, but I knew that my mother knew how to handle the money. She taught us how to be frugal, how to shop properly. Jack and I have been frugal all of our lives.

We learned that part of being frugal was spending our money wisely. Our parents taught us never buy anything and then pay for it. Always save your money before you buy. If you don't have the money to pay cash for something, don't buy it. The only exception is your home. When you get married and you buy a piece of furniture, don't you buy it and put it on credit. Don't you buy it and pay if off over three years. You save the money, then buy it.

Do Americans need to hear that today? Yes! Americans need to hear that today because we have a savings emergency. Do you realize that in this 21st century we've already had two years where we've recorded negative savings in this country? In 2005, we saved .5%. The year 2005 was the worst savings year since the Great Depression.

Whatever you have, spend less.
– Samuel Johnson

LESSON 6

BE PLEASANT, BE NICE TO PEOPLE

My mom died in our house with Janet and me at 92 years of age. Right up until the day she died, she was pleasant. She never complained. In addition to being pleasant, she taught us to be nice to people.

Nobody wants to associate with negative people. Good manners have attraction power.

Jack learned this lesson better than I did. He holds to the belief that everybody wears a badge that reads, "Think well of me, encourage me."

Life is not so short but that there is always time enough for courtesy.
– Ralph Waldo Emerson

Jack and Garry pictured with Mom late in her life.

LESSON 7

SPEND SEVERAL HOURS A DAY READING

Unlike Dad, Mom was well educated. She had two years of college, which was really something back in those days, particularly for a female. Mom was a reader. She'd instruct us, "You need to spend time reading." She would read the newspaper cover to cover. She'd read books. I learned from my mother to spend several hours every day reading.

As many of you know, we subscribe to the philosophy that, "readers are leaders and leaders are readers." We try to read all the biographies we can, particularly on people like Lincoln, Churchill, Reagan and Robert E. Lee – all great leaders. We read out of the King James version of the Bible. We've read books by Napoleon Hill, W. Clement Stone, Zig Ziglar, Charlie "Tremendous" Jones, Maxwell Maltz, and Fred Smith, just to name a few. We'll talk more about this when we get to Lesson #23.

To open a book brings profit.

WHAT I LEARNED FROM MY BROTHER

LESSON 8

SYSTEMATIZE EVERYTHING

Jack had coached for three years and then he went full time with Equitable (now AXA) selling in our hometown. While I was still in college, I was an intern with Equitable and didn't go full time until I graduated.

I made the Million Dollar Round Table (MDRT) early in my career. It took Jack forever to make the MDRT. One of the reasons being, he was a coach. He had a good market, but he had never been in sales.

When we both became district managers, I started in Bloomington, Illinois, a white-collar college town. Bloomington had two great universities: Illinois Wesleyan and Illinois State. Jack went into management in Mt. Vernon, Illinois. In the 1950s, Mt. Vernon was a desolate part of the state.

After two years in management, I looked around and nobody was following me. I'd hired a lot of good people – captain of the football team, National Honor Society students, president of the student body. I had the best-looking recruits you'd ever want to lay your eyes on, but I couldn't find them. They had all left; they were gone.

Meanwhile, Jack was down in Mt. Vernon building a great organization. He had a crowd following him. One day I went down to see Jack so I could find out what was going on in Mt. Vernon. I told him, "I have the best prospects; you have the best retention. You have a crowd following you; I don't have anybody following me. What are we doing differently?"

I'll tell you what Jack was doing; he was teaching everybody a system. Jack had a system for everything. Jack taught me how to be systems-oriented as a manager. **If he hadn't done this, I would have failed in management.** As it was, I became the #1 district manager in the country for Equitable in Bloomington, all because of this valuable lesson I learned from my brother.

When Jack was in college he wrote a book called, *Coaching Baseball.* He had a system for every part of the game. Several colleges adopted the book as their textbook on how to coach baseball. It was written for college students who were getting ready to go into coaching.

Just as Jack had a system for everything in baseball, he also had a system for everything in management and selling.

- ◆ What you say when you contact people

- ◆ What you say when they object

- ◆ What you say the first two minutes of an interview

- ◆ Fact-finding questions to use

- ◆ How to get a money commitment

- ◆ He had a system for keeping score called the Travel Guide. Today, we call it the Progress Guide.

What was my system? "Get out there and SELL."

And what were my instructions? "You're not having enough interviews. That's your problem. Get out there and sell!"

And as they would be going out the door, they would shout back, "HOW? How do you see the people? What do you say?"

Jack was teaching them a system for everything. I learned from Jack to systematize everything as it relates to selling and management.

Make your process so simple that when ordinary people follow it, they perform in an extraordinary fashion.

LESSON 9
YOU PLAY LIKE YOU PRACTICE

Jack loved to tell his players, "You play like you practice." He brought that into the insurance business. He would tell those young agents, "You play like you practice." In our industry, that means you better role play. You better know your script, because you're going to play like you practice. Jack is a master at getting people to play like they practice.

When Jack's daughter Jayne was selling for Xerox she'd occasionally stop by our office. Sometimes it'd be after a big sale, and sometimes she'd come for coaching. While she'd be explaining the problem to Jack, he'd be making his way around to the front of his desk. Before Jayne knew it, Jack would have her engaged in role play, going over and over the basics of the selling process. It wouldn't be long before the solution was uncovered and she'd be on her way to the next sales call.

You play like you practice!

I was a guy who practiced until the blisters bled,
and then practiced some more.
When I was a kid I carried my bat to class with me.
I'd run a buddy's newspaper route if I could get him to shag flies for me.
When I played for San Diego, I paid kids to shag flies on my days off.
– Ted Williams

Garry – left-handed hitting catcher.
Learned from Jack: You play like you practice.

LESSON 10
KEEP YOUR EYE ON THE BALL (PAY ATTENTION)

Being a coach, Jack would tell his players, "Keep your eye on the ball." In golf, baseball, football, you really have to keep your eye on the ball.

When I watch my young granddaughters play basketball, I tell them, "You're not keeping your eye on the ball, you're keeping your eye on the person you're guarding. Keep your eye on the ball."

In the insurance business, that means pay attention. In sales, paying attention is one of the most important qualities to be developed.

We say there are three things you need in this business:

- The first is character, basic integrity.

- Secondly, you need discipline – the discipline to do what you ought to do.

- The third is the trait of paying attention. You want to listen intently to everything the prospect is saying. Some agents come out of an interview and they didn't hear half of what was said, or if they heard it, they didn't hear the right thing. You need to pay attention to what the prospect says. Pay attention to what the prospect didn't say. Pay attention to body language; many times, this reveals more than words.

Jack taught me to pay attention. He always said, "Don't look, see something. Don't listen, hear something. Pay attention."

When you really listen to what prospects are saying, it makes your use of questions more productive; you will uncover what they are not saying. When you uncover what they are not saying, you have helped them discover what they needed to say, but didn't know how.

Listening is magic in selling.
– Frank Bettger

WHAT I LEARNED FROM MY EARLY PASTORS

Lesson 11

Dr. Zimmerman taught me I could be a force for good or a force for evil

We went to the same small church my mother attended when she was a little girl. In that small town, it was a tremendous church. It had a gymnasium – a full basketball court, which was unheard of in those days.

We'd go there on Saturday mornings and play basketball. We'd bring our friends over – members and non-members. We'd have a good time.

I was probably a little bit more ornery than I should have been. One day the pastor called me over and said, "You know, Garry, you're a leader. You're a born leader. You're already captain of the basketball team in junior high. Let me tell you something, young man, you can be a force for good or a force for evil. Right now, you're a force for evil. You're leading people the wrong way. You better shape up. You better make up your mind whether you want to be a force for evil or a force for good."

That made a big impression on me. It was then I decided I was going to be a force for good. I was going to use my leadership skills to lead people to the good things in life.

That pastor helped me have a significant religious experience.

The only thing necessary for the triumph of evil
is for good men to do nothing.
– Edmund Burke

LESSON 12

DR. MARTIN TOLD ME I COULD DO MORE AS A LAYMAN THAN AS A PASTOR

In college, I was in a fraternity. I was president of Phi Gamma Delta (a Figi). We had a dorm in our fraternity house, which meant we spent nine months every year with the same group of college students – fraternity brothers. We'd study together, we'd party together. My fraternity brothers would see me reading the Bible daily, and from time to time they would say to me, "You know, Garry, you ought to be a pastor – that's what you ought to do – be a preacher." That weighed heavily on my mind.

My mother always told me, "Garry, I want you to be a preacher." In my mother's eyes, Jack was going to be a coach and I was going to be a preacher. I never thought that way in my mind; I never felt that way in my heart.

One day, I decided to go see Dr. Martin privately at his home. Dr. Martin was the pastor at the church I attended when I was in college. I told him my problem. "My mom has always told me I need to be a preacher, my fraternity brothers say it, others tell me the same thing." Dr. Martin quickly responded, "Forget that! You would know it if you were called, and you're not called. You can do more good as a layman, as a successful businessman, than you could ever do as a preacher."

So I learned from Dr. Martin that I could do more good for people as a layman than I could as a professional preacher. This half-hour session in Dr. Martin's home had a tremendous impact on my life.

Today, after 50 years in the life insurance industry, people still make these same comments. I always give the same answer, "I can do more good as a layman than I ever could as a pastor. I'm right where I need to be."

*To be successful, you have to have your heart in your business
and your business in your heart.*
– Thomas Watson, Sr.

Garry speaking in Hawaii with Churchill book in his hand – 2006

WHAT I LEARNED FROM MY COACHES

Lesson 13

I learned more on the playing field than I ever did in the classroom

Jack and I were both members of the National Honor Society in high school. We took our schoolwork seriously. We had tremendous high school teachers who prepared us well for college. Even so, I can say without fear of equivocation that I learned more on the playing field than I ever learned in the classroom.

As a freshman in high school, Jack learned fundamentals from Coach John Moss. Five years later when I came along as a freshman, Coach Moss drilled into me those same fundamentals. We teach fundamentals to agents and managers today. We coach them to stay brilliant on the basics.

Jim Lewis was my varsity coach in basketball and football. Coach Lewis taught us to be winners. I was fortunate enough to be on a varsity basketball team as a sophomore. We were in the "Sweet 16" in Illinois two of my three years on the team. I learned how to win.

One of my greatest coaches was Jack Kinder, my brother. In 1950, under Jack's coaching, we were Junior Legion State Champs. He took us within one game of being in the Junior Legion National Championships. We were beat out by a team from Fargo, North Dakota.

The following year, my high school baseball team went on to be the Illinois State Champs under Coach Harry Anderson. Coach Anderson was a professional baseball player. He taught us how to play baseball in a professional manner.

One of my college coaches was Jack Horenberger. He coached me in basketball and in baseball. The main thing I learned from him was to be calm, cool and collected.

Coach Bert Bertonelli was my college football coach. He taught us to pay the price, to be disciplined in everything we did. We were privileged to have the first undefeated football team in the history of Illinois Wesleyan University.

One must learn by doing the thing, for though you think you know it, you have no certainty until you try.
– Aristotle

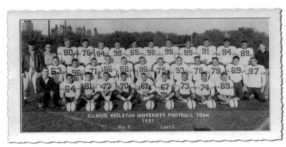

Garry's undefeated college team. Garry is #67

High School Baseball State Champions

Junior Legion State Champs

Lesson 14

I learned teamwork

One of the important things I learned on the playing field was teamwork. If you are going to win, you have to have the involvement of all the team members.

This is true in the game of life. You can't do it alone. Whether it's sports or life, being a member of a team builds a bond that gives you the confidence to accomplish great goals, not only as a team, but also individually.

Garry, #24, at age 15, sophomore in high school,
playing with a team that came in fifth in the state tournament.

Alone we can do so little; together we can do so much.
– Helen Keller

LESSON 15

I LEARNED THE MOST IMPORTANT WORD IN THE ENGLISH LANGUAGE: DISCIPLINE

Jack and I became very disciplined athletes. This carried over into our personal lives and into the business world. We developed the discipline to do what we ought to do.

In 1940, Albert E.N. Gray delivered a great speech at the National Association of Life Underwriters (NALU)* meeting in Philadelphia. This is where he introduced the famous "Common Denominator of Success." The essence of his speech was "Successful people form the habits of doing the things failing people don't like to do." We form habits through the key word in life, which is discipline.

Whether it's a student in college, an athlete in the professional ranks, or an adviser in the financial services world, we all need to form habits through self-discipline to do the things failures don't like to do.

Failing students don't like to study, failing professional athletes don't like to practice, failing people in the financial services world don't like to make contacts, memorize scripts or keep good records.

Discipline is a tremendous characteristic that we learned on the playing field. We learned that champions possess the discipline to practice when nobody is watching. We learned to stay focused when the going gets tough during the heat of battle.

*NALU is known today as NAIFA

We must all suffer from one of two pains:
the pain of discipline or the pain of regret.
The difference is discipline weighs ounces
while regret weighs tons.
– Jim Rohn

Going to a St. Louis Cardinals game with Dad.
Yes, we were Cardinals fans!

WHAT I LEARNED FROM
MY FRATERNITY BROTHERS

Lesson 16

I LEARNED MORE FROM MY FRATERNITY BROTHERS THAN I DID IN THE CLASSROOM

One of the highlights of my college career was being the backup quarterback as a freshman for the first undefeated football team in Illinois Wesleyan University's history. What a thrill this was for a young 18-year-old playing with mainly 25- and 26-year-old men returning from the Korean War.

Another great thrill in college came when I was elected president of the Phi Gamma Delta fraternity. This was an exciting time for me and a time of growth.

There's no question, I learned more from my fraternity brothers than I did from my professors, and I had some great college professors.

The same is true in our business. Agents learn more about selling out in the field than they ever do in the training class. The necessity and value of joint selling cannot be overemphasized.

The great aim of education is not knowledge, but action.

Lesson 17

I LEARNED HOW TO GET ALONG WITH ALL TYPES OF PEOPLE

When you live in the fraternity house three years and you spend 24 hours a day with college friends, you learn a lot about people. It's down and dirty.

We ate two formal meals every day, one at lunch and the other at dinner. We were taught etiquette and good manners.

There were two bathrooms for 40 fraternity brothers; we learned to share!

This experience taught me how to get along with all kinds of people, in all kinds of circumstances. My fraternity brothers taught me many things I needed to learn about people skills and social skills.

The most important single ingredient in the formula of success is knowing how to get along with people.
– Theodore Roosevelt

Doyle Glass, Dad, Garry, Gary Newell, Jack – all from Pekin – friends and teammates

LESSON 18

I LEARNED TO SACRIFICE FOR THE GOOD OF THE CAUSE

There's always competition among fraternities, and ours was no different. We competed against the other Greek fraternities in everything. We competed against them in intramural athletics, we competed with them academically. We were ranked in regard to leadership on campus.

The school had an annual Greek Songfest. Now, singing a song in a contest did not excite me in the least. I was told that as president of the fraternity I had to participate, whether I liked it or not. After they heard me sing a few times, they asked me to just "mouth" the words.

Having to participate in these songfests taught me the importance of sacrificing for the good of the cause. We can't always do just what we want to do. There are sacrifices to be made in family life and in the business world.

In this world it is not what we take up,
but what we give up, that makes us rich.
– Henry Ward Beecher

WHAT I LEARNED FROM MY LIFE INSURANCE PROFESSOR

LESSON 19

BE A STUDENT OF THE BUSINESS

My life insurance instructor was Dr. William T. Beadles. Many of you have studied under Dr. Beadles. He has written many books for Chartered Life Underwriter (CLU) students. Dr. Beadles was a close friend of Dr. Solomon Huebner. They were two peas in a pod.

You go to the American College in Bryn Mawr, Pennsylvania, today and there's a building dedicated to Dr. William T. Beadles. He and Dr. Huebner graded the first CLU exam ever taken. Think about it for a moment. When they first started, CLU tests were five modules, 100% essay. They were taken at the same hour everywhere across the country. They started at 11 a.m. on the east coast, 8 a.m. on the west coast – all essay! It was a four-hour exam. Can you imagine grading all those essay tests and giving a pass or a fail – unbelievable!

Half of the books that Jack and I have written are dedicated to Dr. William T. Beadles. We did this because of his influence on us. He wasn't just a great life insurance professor, he was a great professor. He has had a tremendous influence on this industry. From Dr. Beadles, I learned to be a student of the business.

What else did I learn from this great man? Take a look at Lessons #20, 21 and 22.

This is the way of the most wise and useful people –
the more they know, the more they long to know.
– Dale Dauten

LESSON 20

BUY ALL THE LIFE INSURANCE THE COMPANY WILL ISSUE

Dr. Beadles would always say, "How much life insurance should you own?" Then he would answer his own question and say, "As much as the company will issue!"

He was saying this to young college students. They were studying a course called life insurance, a three-hour course, a tough course. Some of these students were going into the life insurance business, some were going to work for home offices, but most were not. In general, they were students who were in the business school and they were getting three more hours of credit studying a product called life insurance.

You want to buy all the permanent life insurance the company will issue. They'll underwrite you physically, morally, and they'll underwrite you financially. They will not let you buy more than you can handle. You can just put on the app where it says amount: "Issue as much as possible."

Life insurance is really nothing but money.
You don't need more life insurance, but you do need more money.
If you live, we call it thrift; when you die, we call it life insurance.

Lesson 21
Always buy permanent life insurance

Dr. Huebner and Dr. Beadles would be turning over in their graves right now if they knew the way we were handling term insurance in this country. I can close my eyes and remember Dr. Beadles saying, "Term insurance is designed to cover bank loans. Term insurance was never designed for the buying public."

If you go back and look at the amount of term insurance that was bought in the '40s, '50s and the early '60s, it was insignificant. Nobody had money, but when they bought life insurance, they bought permanent life insurance.

Today, we're "term insurancing" this country to death. According to Life Insurance Marketing and Research Association (LIMRA) statistics, it's getting worse, not better. More and more people have less and less life insurance. And of the life insurance they own personally, more and more of it is term insurance.

You can't solve a permanent problem with temporary insurance.

LESSON 22

MAKE DECISIONS ON HOW THEY ARE GOING TO AFFECT YOU 15 YEARS FROM TODAY

Dr. Beadles said, "Make all major decisions based on how they will affect you 15 years from today. Do this and you'll make very few mistakes."

Why?

Because stopping to consider the long-term consequences of any action is basic to choosing wisely. If you have a major decision to make, it becomes even more important that you weigh the outcome with your long-term goals and dreams in mind. This also helps you determine just how important the decision really is. Does it matter in the long run?

Once you make a decision, make it right. Stick to it!

…until a person can say deeply and honestly,
"I am what I am today because of the choices I made yesterday,"
that person cannot say, "I choose otherwise."
– Steven Covey

WHAT I LEARNED FROM
EARL NIGHTINGALE

The Great Earl Nightingale

As a college student selling life insurance, I encountered the great Earl Nightingale. Jack and I learned many lessons from him early in our insurance career. Here's what I learned!

Lesson 23

Ideas and Concepts are what Change People's Lives

This statement had a phenomenal impact on my life. I couldn't get it out of my mind. When I first learned it, I was a very young man and I asked myself the question, "How do you sell life insurance?" Remember, when I was asking myself that question, there was no such thing as a computer printout. All we had were rate books.

REMEMBER RATE BOOKS?! We had big ones and small ones. Our managers would tell us, "Don't you ever lose it, because we can't replace it. In five years we're going to create a new one, but until then, don't lose it. Guard it with your life. Sleep with it under your pillow."

Did we sell with rate books? NO! We sold with ideas and concepts. Today, we need to be selling with ideas, concepts, stories and pictures.

By the way, that's the way you recruit. You don't recruit with numbers. You need to know the numbers, but you don't recruit with them. Recruit with ideas, concepts, stories and pictures.

I learned this lesson in the late '50s from Earl Nightingale. Then, in the late '70s, I was on a program in Niagara Falls, Canada – 3,500 people in attendance – at the time, the biggest crowd I'd ever spoken to. I was following Norman Vincent Peale on the program. As I sat there listening, midway through his presentation he said, "Ideas and concepts are what change civilizations." He said Hitler turned this world upside down with one idea – demolish the Jews. When Hitler said this, he meant wipe them off the face of the earth. Do we have any people trying to do that today? We have world leaders whose announced goal is to destroy the Jews.

On a positive note, President John F. Kennedy said, "We can get to the moon in this decade." He turned this country upside down. We were on kind of a plateau, but President Kennedy's idea changed us completely. This country went to work, and look at the revolution that happened in our space program. The technology resulting from the space program has given us the global communication we enjoy today. We have seen advances in medical technology. Many of the tools and safety devices we enjoy in our homes today are the result of the research done through the space program. Black & Decker cordless tools and smoke detectors are among those.

As a young man, I thought Earl Nightingale was the first person to ever say, "Ideas and concepts are what change people's lives." I later discovered it was Plato who said, "Ideas have consequences."

Let me ask you, when I was a young boy, where did I get my ideas? I got my ideas from my mom, dad, older brother and – where else – my church! Today, where are young kids getting their ideas? TV, the Internet, video games. There's been a dramatic change in our country!

Feed your mind good thoughts, good ideas. Pass on positive thoughts and ideas to your family and friends.

Ideas and concepts change lives and civilizations.

An invasion of armies can be resisted,
but not an idea whose time has come.
– Victor Hugo

LESSON 24

READ ONE GOOD BOOK EVERY MONTH ON HOW TO LIVE AND HOW TO WORK

Another great lesson Earl Nightingale taught us is that you should read one good book every month on how to live and how to work. He said, "The educational system you came out of taught you everything but how to live and how to work. You have to get that on your own." Two important things, you have to get them on your own.

As I shared with you in Lesson 7, my mom had introduced this lesson early on: Spend time reading every day. This lesson from Earl Nightingale taught us to read with purpose.

Right up until Jack had a stroke, he would read one good book a week. Today, Jack still reads by listening to books on tape.

The man who doesn't read good books
has no advantage over the man who can't read them.
– Mark Twain

Jack and Garry with Roger Staubach
when they wrote Winning Strategies in Selling.

LESSON 25

GOOD STUFF IN, GOOD STUFF OUT;
BAD STUFF IN, BAD STUFF OUT

Another thing Earl Nightingale always said was that your brain is like a computer. You put good stuff in, good stuff is going to come out. You put bad stuff in, bad stuff is going to come out. He'd say, "Good stuff in, good stuff out – MULTIPLIED!"

He loved to quote Emerson who was really quoting the Bible, "As ye sow, so shall ye reap – MULTIPLIED! When you plant corn, you're never going to get apples. When you plant apple seeds, you're never going to get corn. As ye sow, so shall ye reap – MULTIPLIED!"

He's also the guy who coined the phrase, "Turn your automobile into a learning center." Instead of getting in your car and turning on the music or news, turn on something that you have proactively chosen to put into your mind.

Rule your mind or it will rule you!

WHAT I LEARNED FROM
THE FINANCIAL
SERVICES INDUSTRY

LESSON 26

WINNERS KEEP ON WINNING; LOSERS KEEP ON LOSING

Generally speaking, winners keep on winning. Successful people keep on being successful.

I don't quite understand this, and I'm not going to tell you I have the answers, however, I have observed that winners win and losers lose. Winners keep on winning, and losers keep on losing.

Automobile insurance companies have built their rates on this principle. It's a little overstated, but it's still a truism.

Bet on the winners because they keep on winning. Stay away from losers because they keep on losing.

Winning is a habit.

Garry, Jim Sundberg, Roger Staubach, Mike Hargrove and Jack

LESSON 27

NOTHING IS AS CONSTANT AS CHANGE

Jack and I learned this from our first manager, Fred Holderman. He taught us many great management principles. He always said, "Nothing is as constant as change."

Are things changing in this world? Are things changing in your world? Are things going to continue to change? They're changing. And the change is coming faster all the time. The older we get, the more we need to learn to handle change.

Dr. O.S. Hawkins taught us some things always change; some things never change. Methods change all the time, the message rarely changes.

In a world of constant change, you need unchanging principles. Here are a few messages Mr. Holderman taught us that haven't changed:

(1) **As an agent, you are the home office's representative to the client – and you're also the client's representative to the home office.** You must treat both parties on an equal basis – fairly and impartially. You should not expect any advantages for either. If you do not know exactly how the home office will treat a subject, be sure to make this clear to the client. Whenever the home office has the wrong impression of a client, do not fail to be aggressive in your endeavor to give them the true picture.

(2) **Listen to learn.** This eliminates a lot of disappointments. Listen, and you'll learn – only then will you be ready to win.

(3) **Maintain a positive attitude.** This is an absolute. Do this on a consistent basis, and it will guarantee your success.

(4) **Always be accountable.** Achieve accountability and you'll maximize productivity.

(5) **You can't lose something you never had.** This pertains to competitive selling. When a prospective client goes with another company, keep in mind you didn't lose the client – you never had the client.

(6) **Do not crowd the truth in any of your statements.**

(7) **Be a good manager of finances.** You'll have many temptations to spend extra money. Your credit will be good because of your income. Use good judgment. Carefully manage outgo against income.

Change is not made without inconvenience,
even from worse to better.
– Samuel Johnson

LESSON 28 ════════════════════════

CHANGE IS INEVITABLE, GROWTH IS OPTIONAL

The rate of change is accelerating dramatically. The computer chip has changed our world. Electronics have really helped our industry.

We cannot predict what the future changes will be, however, we can predict with 100% accuracy that there will be change. Whether or not we accept, develop and grow with change is optional.

> *Results improve to the extent that the leader*
> *embraces change and makes change positive.*
> – David Cottrell

LESSON 29 ════════════════════════

MEMORIZE THE SCRIPTS; AD LIBS ARE FOR AMATEURS

Memorize the scripts. I learned this from many people, not the least of which was my brother. He preached this principle on a regular basis.

When Jack started in the business, Fred Holderman had a script that all the new agents learned. I can remember this like it was yesterday. Jack would give me the script and, in the front room of our house, he would sit me down and say, "Garry, I want you to watch this script and make sure I don't miss one word."

The script was about four or five pages, and here was Jack having me make sure he wasn't missing a word. He said, "If I miss a word, you stop me." I'd say, "Jack, you missed a word. You added something it doesn't say." I did that with him all summer. Before long, I knew the script as well as he did.

When I started one year later as a part-time agent, it didn't take me long to memorize the script because I'd been helping Jack. Today, if you turn to page 87 in our book, *Secrets of Successful Insurance Sales*, you'll find about half of that script modernized. The key words go like this:

> *"Rather than come to you today and tell you that you need this or that, quote you some prices, and sell you something on that basis, we at Equitable, in situations like yours do the opposite.*
>
> *"We ask you, 'Have you made provisions in your life insurance and investment programs to maximize your monthly pension income when you retire? At your death, what sort of income do you want guaranteed to your family? What do you want done with the mortgage on your home if something happens to you? If you become sick or are injured, and can't work, what sort of income will you need? What sort of education do you want for your son or daughter?'*
>
> *"We take your responses to these and similar questions back to our office. There we study, analyze, and review your situation. With the assistance of our computer support, we individualize your case and personalize a recommendation for your consideration. In a few days, we return and give you our recommendation. If you like it, we'd like to have you as a client. However, you're under no obligation."*

Remember, I was learning all of this from helping Jack memorize it, and I wasn't even in the business.

It continues by saying,

> *"Now here is what I would like to do."* (Lean forward and lower your voice.) *"I'd like to gather this information. I'd like to pick up your policies. I'll take all of this to my office, where we will individualize your case. We will study your income and your obligations. We will review the insurance you already own and what it's doing for you. We will then prepare our personalized recommendation.*
>
> *"When I return, I'll give you some information and ideas that will be helpful to you now and in the future. No obligation, of course.*
>
> *"Now, Bill, that's fair enough, isn't it?"* (Nod your head to assist your prospect in making a positive response.)

MEMORIZE YOUR SCRIPTS – AD LIBS ARE FOR AMATEURS.

I always like to tell this story. It's a true story, and it happens to me often. I'll go into an agency and we'll have all these young people around and I'll tell them to memorize the scripts. Invariably, when I tell them to do that, a young agent will come up to me and say, "You know you talk about memorizing scripts, but the scripts don't sound like me." I say, "Those scripts don't sound like you?" He says, "No." I say, "That's good. If they sounded like you, they wouldn't work! Who said they were supposed to sound like you? They're not supposed to sound like you. Here's what you do: First, you MEMORIZE, then you PROFESSIONALIZE, THEN you PERSONALIZE. Then, you know what? They'll sound like you!"

That's what we need to say to young people.

I will prepare and my time will come.
– Abraham Lincoln

LESSON 30

SUCCESSFUL PEOPLE FORM HABITS OF DOING THINGS FAILING PEOPLE DON'T DO

This was first introduced to you in Lesson 15. It was given to us by Albert E.N. Gray in 1940. It's probably at the top of all the concepts I've learned. It certainly has to be in the top five.

Successful people form the habits of doing the things that failing people don't like to do. He delivered this at a NALU meeting in 1940 in Philadelphia. His first few words went something like this:

I'm Vice President of Sales at Prudential. My problem is, I don't know anything about sales; I'm actuary. But being an actuary, I wanted to find out what it was that every person who had ever been successful at Prudential had in common. Since I am an actuary, I went searching for the common denominator – and I found it. It's as simple as it sounds – it's as true as it seems: Successful people form the habits to do the things failing people don't like to do.

You know what happened there that day? Albert E.N. Gray not only gave us the common denominator for success in sales, he also gave us the common denominator for success in life itself. What is it that failing students in college don't like to do? Study! What is it failing athletes in college and the professional ranks don't like to do? Practice! You go into any area of life and you will find that those who are successful have formed the habits of doing the things that the failures in that area don't like to do.

Habit is like a cable. We weave a strand each day
until it is so strong it cannot be broken.
— Horace Mann

Jack, Olympic champion Frank Shorter and Garry

Lesson 31

Take care of your clients; eventually your clients will take care of you

Please permit me to tell you a very personal story. Four years ago, three of my golfing friends, who are all clients, said, "We're going to take you to dinner Saturday night." This was in September. I said, "What's up?" "Well, we'll tell you when we go to dinner."

So, Saturday night comes and we all meet at this nice restaurant for dinner and I said, "What's going on here?"

It wasn't unusual for all of us to go to dinner, but it was unusual to pick a date, 10 days in advance, pick a nice spot and a private room. As the evening progressed, they produced for me my schedule for the next 12 months. They said, "Do you see the month of May? We want you to know we've talked with your staff and your assistant and we've blocked out 10 days where you are not going to go anywhere. You are going with us, you and Janet. We're going on a 10-day trip. You won't know until the moment we pick you up where we're going. You will need your golf clubs; it'll be a nice temperature. You'll need your passport."

Well, we flew to Paris, then on to Italy to a little community called Abano. We stayed there at a spa for 10 days. They said, "This is an all-expenses-paid trip for you. The three of us are doing this for you and Janet because of what you've done for us." The men golfed; the women shopped. We had a great time!

You take care of your clients, and some day your clients will take care of you.

At this writing, it's been eight months since Jack had a stroke. The outpouring from our personal friends has been a real blessing. The support from our colleagues in this great business is overwhelming.

Take care of your clients, and your clients will eventually take care of you.

Never forget a customer. Never let a customer forget you.

MORE LESSONS FROM
THE FINANCIAL
SERVICES INDUSTRY

Lesson 32

It's always better to pay too much than to pay too little

In almost everything you do, this principle applies. Pay too little financially, or pay too little in terms of time and effort, and the result is the same: You get what you pay for.

In my experience, I have found that if you don't give the project the time it deserves, you pay dearly for it down the line. The same is true in hiring staff. If you try to get by on skimpy wages, you'll pay a bigger price for it at a later date.

This sets the stage for the next two lessons.

It takes time to succeed because success is merely
the natural reward of taking time to do anything well.
— Joseph Ross, Author

Lesson 33

Pay too much, you lose a little money; pay too little, you could lose everything

That's true when you buy insurance. You buy term insurance, you save a little. Most people lose all they paid in premiums. That's true when you buy an automobile. It's true when you buy furniture. It's true when you buy clothes.

Risk comes from not knowing what you're doing.
– Warren Buffett

LESSON 34

WHEN BUYING CLOTHES, PAY TWICE AS MUCH, BUY HALF AS MANY

When I graduated from college, I needed a new suit to go into business. Back in those days, you had two pairs of shoes – Sunday shoes and everyday shoes. Most people like me had one suit. You had a couple of ties and a couple of shirts. That's about it.

I went down to one of the finest men's clothing stores in Bloomington, Illinois. I had just graduated from college and there were many things I needed to take care of financially. I told the clothier I needed a real good suit, but I couldn't pay very much money. He said, "Garry, let me tell you something about buying suits – always pay twice as much and buy half as many. When you buy clothes, you pay twice as much, you buy half as many. They'll stay in style longer, they'll look better and you will always look professional."

Package yourself properly.
Invest twice as much and buy half as many.

Jack and Garry as young executives.

LESSON 35

SPECTACULAR ACHIEVEMENTS COME FROM UNSPECTACULAR PREPARATION

Planning and preparation are always inglorious. No one is clapping, no one is cheering. Planning always comes before the doing, and it is never spectacular.

Being from Pekin, Illinois, we were always thrilled with the remarks of Sen. Everett M. Dirkson. He was the Republican Whip in the senate for many years.

One time a *Chicago Tribune* editor posed this question to the great senator, "You've been the confidant of four presidents, you've known the great and near great in this world. Who would you say is the greatest person alive today?"

Without hesitation, the senator said, "It's somebody you never heard about before. It's a mother who gets up and gets her children prepared for school, it's a farmer down in southern Illinois that goes out and plows the ground with nobody cheering, nobody supervising."

This is the way it is with planning and preparation – no one cheering, no one applauding. You have to do it behind closed doors. Anytime you experience a spectacular achievement, you can attribute it to unspectacular, inglorious preparation.

Lesson 35, Spectacular performance is always preceded by unspectacular preparation.

> *It's not the will to win, but the will to prepare to win*
> *that makes the difference.*
> – Bear Bryant

LESSON 36
THINK ABOUT THE SOLUTION, NOT THE PROBLEM

The great golfers always say, "Don't look at the sand traps, look at the greens. Don't look at the water, look at the pin." Look at the solution, not the problem.

W. Clement Stone said, "With every problem there is sown the seed of an equivalent success." Always look for the solution – always look for the better things in life.

In 1983, I was privileged to help my son-in-law, Curt Ladd, get started in this great business. I told him, "Don't walk away from negative people – RUN AWAY!! You are going to get enough negatives conducting your business day in and day out. You don't need negatives from people in the office or from friends. So don't walk away from negative people – run away!"

You want to think about the solution, not the problem.

> *The "how" thinker gets problems solved effectively*
> *because he wastes no time with futile "ifs"*
> *but goes right to work on the creative "how."*
> – Norman Vincent Peale

LESSON 37

GREAT PERFORMERS DO NOT WAIT FOR INSPIRATION

Great performers get up and get the job done. Let me give you two examples – Winston Churchill and Abraham Lincoln. They have been called by many people the greatest leaders of the last 500 years.

Dr. Billy Graham says they are the two greatest leaders of the last 2,000 years. He gave it a biblical overtone when he said, "They're the two greatest leaders since the Apostle Paul."

Both of them fought serious depression every day of their lives. Both of them spoke with clarity, and both of them kept it simple. They didn't wait for inspiration; they just got up every day and got the job done.

At 80, late in his life, Churchill made this observation, "I have noticed that people getting the job done in this world are people that don't feel good."

We say feelings always follow actions. If you get into action, you'll feel better. Salespeople need to understand, feelings always follow actions.

It's not enough that we do our best;
sometimes we have to do what's required.
– Winston Churchill

LESSON 38

SHOW UP ON TIME, DRESSED, READY TO PLAY

Show up on time, dressed, ready to play. We learned that from Dr. Michael Mescon. Here's the way he dramatizes it: "If you just **show up**, you're going to have 75% of the people in this world beat. If you **show up on time**, now you have 90% of the people beat. If you **show up on time, dressed, ready to play,** you'll have them all beat. That's the way to be successful." That's what he would tell his young students getting ready to go out into the business world. That's the way you become highly successful.

There are two kinds of people in the world:
Those who are always getting ready to do something,
and those who go ahead and do it.

Lesson 39

Make every occasion a great occasion

Make every occasion a great occasion for you never know who's taking your measure for a higher position in life.

Every occasion – even an unwanted, time-consuming interruption – can be transformed into a great occasion. How? Simply by viewing the event through the lens of an expectant, creative attitude.

A prospect calls and cancels an appointment at the last minute. A great occasion? Hardly! But wait! Turn that temporary "rejection" into a reward. Use those few free minutes to take stock of the situation.

Remember this truth: There are always other sources. There are always other prospects, customers and clients. The salesperson who realizes this will inevitably grow from anxiety to confidence, from fear to courage in the face of fear, and from pessimism to productivity.

Depending on our attitude toward them, interruptions can:

♦ be viewed as sources of irritation or opportunities for service,

♦ be viewed as moments lost or experiences gained,

♦ be viewed as time wasted or horizons widened,

♦ annoy us or enrich us,

♦ get under our skin or give us a shot in the arm,

♦ monopolize our minutes or spice our schedules.

No occasion is a "little" occasion. No moment is insignificant in its own way. No person is unimportant in his/her own eyes.

This call – this interruption, this question, this objection, this situation – can be a very great occasion if you choose to make it so!

> *A great individual is made up of qualities*
> *that meet or make great occasions.*
> – James Russell Lowell

LESSON 40
UTILIZE THE WISE COUNSEL OF OTHERS

Everybody needs a mentor. In her book, *We Shall Not Fail*, Winston Churchill's granddaughter Celia Sandys titled one of the chapters, "Find your Clementine." Clementine was Churchill's wife, but she was also his mentor, his confidant. She did not mentor him per se on what to do, but he could talk to her and lay out all of his problems in a way he couldn't do with anyone else.

The book showed handwritten letters she sent him during war time. One of them said, "My Darling, I hope you will forgive me if I tell you something which I feel you ought to know." She went on to say she was upset and astonished to hear he was becoming rough and overbearing. She knew he was under tremendous pressure, but wisely advised he would not get the best results by what she saw as "irascibility and rudeness." She ended, "Please forgive your loving, devoted and watchful Clemmie."

The one thing Jack and I always had going for us is we were each other's counselor.

Develop mentors. Get your advice from successful people.

Jack mentoring Garry.

EVEN MORE LESSONS FROM
THE FINANCIAL
SERVICES INDUSTRY

LESSON 41
NEVER CONFUSE ACTIVITY WITH ACCOMPLISHMENT

The reason for activity is to get results. In the financial services industry, you are paid for results, not for staying busy.

Don't tell me how hard you are working, don't tell me the number of hours you are putting in, don't tell me the number of people you have been seeing. In our business, the results are always the final judge.

Result-producing activities for agents are:

♦ Setting new sales appointments

♦ Closing interviews (ask-to-buys)

Result-producing activities for managers are:

♦ Prospecting for agents

♦ Evaluating prospective agents

♦ Attracting prospective agents

♦ Joint field work with new agents

*There is nothing so useless as doing efficiently
that which should not be done at all.*
– Peter Drucker

Lesson 42

Honest, intelligent effort is always rewarded

Honest effort is *not* always rewarded. *Intelligent effort* is *not* always rewarded. However, *honest, intelligent effort is ALWAYS rewarded.*

Why?

Anybody can put forth a little honest effort on the wrong thing. The reverse is also true; you can have the best-laid plans thought out by the best minds, but without integrity at the core, these plans fail sooner or later.

You need both elements for success – honest effort + intelligent effort = rewards.

Lee J. Colan relates this story in his book, *7 Moments that Define Excellent Leaders.*

> *Two young men were working their way through Stanford University in the late 1890s when, during the semester, their funds got desperately low and they came up with the idea of engaging Ignacy Paderewski, the great pianist, for a recital. After paying the concert expenses, the two students could use the profits to pay their board and tuition.*

> *The great pianist's manager asked for a guarantee of two thousand dollars. The students, undaunted, proceeded to stage the concert. But alas, the concert raised only sixteen hundred dollars.*

> *After the performance, the students sought the great artist, gave him the entire sixteen hundred dollars, a promissory*

note for four hundred dollars and explained they would earn the remainder of his fee and send the money to him.

"No," replied Paderewski, "that won't do." Then, tearing the note to shreds, he returned the money and said to them, "Now, take out of this sixteen hundred dollars all of your expenses and keep for each of you 10 percent of the balance for your work."

The years rolled by – years of fortune and destiny. Paderewski had become Premier of Poland. The devastating war came, and Paderewski's only focus was to feed the starving thousands in his beloved Poland. Yet just as the need was most severe, thousands of tons of food began to come into Poland for distribution by the Polish Premier.

After all the starving people were fed and hard times had past, Paderewski journeyed to Paris to thank Herbert Hoover for the relief he had sent. "That's all right, Mr. Paderewski," was Mr. Hoover's reply. "You don't remember it, but you helped me once when I was a student at college and I was in a hole. You invested in me … now it's my turn."

Always do what's right – no matter what! Honest, intelligent effort is always rewarded.

Always do right; it will gratify some and astonish the rest.
– Mark Twain

LESSON 43

STRATEGIES WON'T WORK UNLESS YOU DO

For many years, we have said any system will work if you will work the system. We feel that some systems are better than others. However, it's not just the system that counts, it's the activity.

It's important to have systems, scripts and strategies. It's far more important, however, to have the right activity with the right people.

The result is the final judge!

Efficiency is doing a thing right.
Effectiveness is doing the right thing.
You must know the difference.

LESSON 44

PROFESSIONALS ARE AT THEIR BEST – REGARDLESS

Always be at your best. You never know who's taking your measure for a higher position in life, including, of course, the purchase of a financial product.

Professionals get up and go to work. They keep on keeping on, no matter what.

Success is for those energetic enough to work for it,
hopeful enough to look for it, patient enough to wait for it,
brave enough to seize it, and strong enough to hold it.

Lesson 45

Don't expect perfection – expect excellence

There's a big difference in the results you get from expecting perfection and expecting excellence.

Expecting perfection paralyzes people. They become afraid to do anything at all for fear of failure. The result is a lot of activity, no results.

This is another one of Jack's specialties. Here's what Jack would always say, "Stamp it with excellence." And that's all he expects of anyone: Excellence, their best.

He modeled this in everything he did. Whether it was at the country club, on the golf course, at the church with his IMPACT Bible Study group, or through the way he lived his everyday life, in everything, he stamped it with excellence.

As a 6-year-old, I remember watching Jack in junior high school. His clothes were immaculate. Even as a teenager, he bought good clothes and was always properly dressed. He stamped it with excellence.

Now, in his speech therapy after having a stroke, Jack is still applying this same attitude – expecting excellence – expecting excellence from himself and the therapists.

Don't expect perfection from yourself. Don't expect perfection from your associates. Expect excellence. Expect them to do their best. If they always strive to be at their best, the results will take care of themselves.

The secret of joy in work is contained in one word – excellence.
To know how to do something well is to enjoy it.
– Pearl S. Buck

Jack and his family celebrating Christmas 2005.

LESSON 46

WHEN PEOPLE STOP GETTING BETTER, THEY CEASE TO BE GOOD

The person who decides to coast is going to coast downhill. You can't coast the bicycle uphill. So the moment you decide to coast in any area of life, you're going downhill.

It's OK to retire. In today's world, people should retire and stay active. Some will go into another business. Some will get active in a charity. Stay active, keep your mind alert.

A mentor and leader of ours, Coy Eklund, is 91 years old and maintains an office. He is very active in his favorite charities. He calls his friends and former associates on a regular basis just to see how they are doing.

Peter Drucker, the great management guru, stayed active right up until the day he died at age 95.

Our good friend, Fred Smith, was still going strong on his 91st birthday. I was there with him. He was passing out philosophies "a mile a minute."

The person who stops getting better, ceases to be good.

Mind is a muscle. Continue to exercise it.
Refuse membership in the "I Used to Be" Club.
– Thomas J. Watson, Jr.

Gary Schulte, Garry, Coy Eklund and Jack

LESSON 47

THERE'S NO SECOND CHANCE TO MAKE A GOOD FIRST IMPRESSION

We've all heard the old cliché, "Don't judge a book by its cover," but we do.

Many people make important judgments, right or wrong, on first impressions. Because most prospects will judge you in the first two minutes of your initial contact, you must look the part, walk the part, talk the part. Watch the way you shake hands – watch your eye contact – watch your dress and demeanor.

On the telephone, your first words are crucial. To maximize your telephone effectiveness, follow a script that you have memorized, professionalized and personalized!

To make a good first impression, focus your attention on the other person. Be sincere and willing to listen. Be positive and enthusiastic. Be the first to speak and introduce yourself.

LESSON 48

DON'T WASTE TIME WITH THOSE WHO WASTE YOUR TIME

Some people are time wasters. I tell young agents if Mr. or Mrs. Client says they want to think it over or they want to compare, hand them your business card and ask them to please give you a call once they've had a chance to think it over or compare.

If they call you, great! If they don't, you haven't wasted your time with someone who was wasting your time.

By the way, they rarely call!

> *Anything that is wasted effort represents wasted time.*
> *The best management of our time thus becomes*
> *linked inseparably with the best utilization of our efforts.*
> – Ted W. Engstrom

WHAT I LEARNED FROM DR. W.A. CRISWELL

Lesson 49

Life is Short, Life is Fragile

First Baptist Church of Dallas had two beloved pastors who served that congregation for 50 years each. One was George W. Truett and the other was Dr. W.A. Criswell. Jack and I and our families were fortunate to have been members of this great church under Dr. Criswell. Our families were also privileged to be led at this church by the great Dr. O.S. Hawkins, who has become a true family friend.

Dr. Criswell baptized all of our family members. He officiated at the weddings of Jack's daughter, Jayne Ann, and our two daughters, Karen and Karol.

Many of you know that in 1990, I lost my wife of 34 years. My wife, Janet, lost her husband to cancer in 1985. When Janet and I were getting married, Dr. Criswell said this to us: "Life is short, life is fragile. Be at your best every day, because you never know."

At 19 years of age, I knew one thing for certain: At some point in the next few years I was going to be a major-league catcher. I knew that in my mind. I believed it in my heart. My mother believed it. My dad believed it. My brother believed it. My coaches believed it.

My mother used to say to me, after she finished telling me to be a preacher, "You know your dad and your brother say some day you're going to be a major-league baseball player." I'd say, "Thanks, Mom. That's what I want to do."

At age 19, I showed up at the Mayo Clinic and, after three days of examination, the doctor was ready to release me. In the exit interview he said, "Young man, let me tell you something as straight as I can tell it to you. You will never play competitive athletics again for the rest of your life. You need to get that through your brain. You have nerve damage in your left hand. You're never going to play competitive athletics again that require the use of a left hand. Now do you understand that?" I said, "Yes, Sir."

The doctor asked me this question: "Do you believe in the Great Physician?" I said, "Yes, sir." He said, "You better start praying, because that hand is so messed up that if it doesn't heal itself in the next nine to 12 months, we're going to have to fuse it. That means you'll not be able to bend your thumb or your fingers for the rest of your life."

Leaving the Mayo Clinic, I knew for the first time in my life that life is short, and life is fragile. I had hit a wall. I had to turn around and go 180 degrees in a different direction. I took all of the passion I had to be a major-league baseball player and focused it all on the life insurance business.

People often ask me, "Why are you so passionate?" My consistent response is, "I'm just a passionate person about things I believe in deeply. I had a passion to play baseball and now I have a passion to promulgate the financial services industry."

At 19, I learned pretty quick that life is short, life is fragile.

In 1990, when I lost my wife of 34 years, I learned again that life is short, life is fragile.

On January 31, 2006, I was getting on a plane to go to Boston. I got a phone call. Jack had suffered a massive stroke. Life is short, life is fragile. You better be at your best every day; you never know.

Some of you reading this book have had something like this happen to you. It may be happening to you right now. You always want to remember that it's not what happens to us that counts, it's how we react to what happens to us that counts. We're not made in a crisis; we are revealed in a crisis.

Attach yourself to your passion, but not to your pain.
Adversity is your best friend on the path to success.

Jack, Mary Sue, Barbara and Garry

LESSON 50

LOVE NEVER DIVIDES, IT ALWAYS MULTIPLIES

When Janet and I were talking to Dr. Criswell the day before our wedding, he was giving us some sage advice about a second marriage. He said, "Your love for one person will never diminish your love for another." He was talking about our spouses who were deceased. He wisely counseled us, "Love never divides, it always multiplies. What this world needs is more love."

Jesus was once asked by a lawyer what was the greatest commandment. "Jesus said unto him, 'Thou shalt love the Lord thy God with all thy heart, and with all thy soul, and with all thy mind. This is the first and great commandment. And the second is like unto it, Thou shalt love thy neighbour as thyself. On these two commandments hang all the law and the prophets'" (Matthew 22:37-40).

Dr. Criswell taught us the greatest lesson of all, Lesson 50: "Love never divides, it always multiplies."

Love never fails.

Janet and Garry

Garry and Janet's wedding – 1992

THE BEST IS YET TO BE!

Take these 50 lessons and use them – put them to work. They are not 50 commandments, they are simply 50 of the best lessons I've learned in 50 years in this great business. I hope they will help you.

When you stay in a business for 50 years you learn many lessons. If you keep your eyes and ears open, you can learn useful principles. As I look back, these are the top 50 things I learned.

Looking forward, I can tell you with all confidence, I have never felt better about this industry than I feel today. Our products are beyond belief. We're working on distribution products in this industry that are going to be completely different – products for people over 70 – life insurance policies for people over 80.

While the future of this industry has never been better, we still have to bring people in who have character and integrity – people with drive, who want to get somewhere. Combine that character, integrity and drive with IQ and common sense, and you have a winner.

For all these reasons, the future has never been brighter in our industry. The next 50 years are shaping up to be better than the last 50. Young people entering this business today can do so with complete confidence: *Money Magazine* recently named the job of financial advisor as the third best in America.

May God bless you and your loved ones, and remember: *The best is yet to be!*

One other great lesson ...

I'd Rather See a Sermon

by Edgar Guest

I'd rather see a sermon than hear one any day;

I'd rather one should walk with me than merely show the way.

The eye's a willing pupil and more willing than the ear,

Fine counsel is confusing, but example's always clear;

And the best of all the leaders are the ones who live their creeds,

For to see the good in action is what everybody needs.

I can soon learn how to do it, if you'll let me see it done;

I can watch your hands in action, but your tongue too fast may run.

And the lectures you deliver, they may be very wise and true,

But I'd rather get my lessons by observing what you do;

For I might misunderstand you and the high advice you give,

But there's no misunderstanding how you act and how you live.

Endorsements

"I've enjoyed over 60 years of true friendship with these two God-centered men, Jack and Garry Kinder. They are the essence of hard work, loyalty, and honesty. Jack and Garry sold me insurance, hired me into the insurance business and led me by example. They have been a tremendous blessing to me my entire life."

Gary Newell
Lifelong Friend
Insurance Broker

"Many of the 50 lessons I learned at the feet of the masters, Jack and Garry Kinder. The lessons have been learned over and over again in business and in life; they are forever."

Dr. Ken Miller
Former President
Grand Canyon University Foundation

"Life has few real heroes and even fewer giants; on rare occasions, they walk among us! The Kinders reveal fundamental cornerstones that are time-tested gems forged from real experience and blessed with divine eternal business principles."

Victor J. Verchereau
Marketing Vice President
Farm Bureau Insurance – MI

"Garry's theme of 'What I learned from … ' parallels my life, and although different chapters, I would like to think after 25 years of studying and following the Kinder principles, I share the same core values that have made the Kinder brothers icons for the Life Insurance Industry."

Steve Ray
Senior Vice President
West Central Agencies
New York Life

"Garry teaches us once again on the philosophies of winning and living a balanced life. Not only required reading but also a book to live by."

Dick Cleary
President and Managing Partner
of The Partners Network – John Hancock

"For more than 25 years Jack and Garry have 'burned it in' with me that I will be no different five years from now except for the books I read, tapes and CDs I listen to, DVDs and videos I watch, and the people I associate with. *50 Lessons in 50 Years* is one of those must-read books that will create enthusiasm for what you do to make a significant contribution in life and help you stay focused on being happy with what you are becoming as a person. This book is about giving and sharing. This is what Garry Kinder reminds us of as we move through this life."

Ron Price
Sr. Vice President, Chief Marketing Officer
Career Life Agencies
American National

"The Kinder brothers have made an enormous contribution to our industry through the years. Garry's '50 Lessons' is a masterpiece on how to achieve success in life and in our business."

Lynn Wilson
Vice President, Life Sales
Farm Bureau Financial Services

"This is a story about a salt-of-the-earth, Midwest, functional family who live the philosophies and actions that have made America great: God, family, country and profession. The pages are filled with wisdom and lessons extolling the importance of positive relationships in families, communities and career. We are all created to reach out to each other for help, for encouragement, for celebration. Jack and Garry Kinder have walked the talk. God bless them!"

Jack Stucko
Director
Corporate Communication/Education Services
Michigan Farm Bureau

"A powerful, concise and intimate look into minds of the greatest insurance management leaders and consultants in the world. Sharing their 50 greatest lessons of leading, teaching, managing and building people gives us all a look into the very heart and soul of the Kinder brothers, Jack and Garry. This is a must-read for every single person in a leadership position in our great industry!"

Kevin P. Kelly
Friend and Regional Director
American National

"*50 Lessons in 50 Years* is an incredible manuscript on life, family, and business – possibly the best example of successful living ever written. It is no wonder the Kinders have become legends in this business and among their families, churches, and friends. This is a masterpiece!"

B. Lee Harrison, Jr., CLU, LUTCF, CLTC
General Agent/CEO
North Florida Financial Corporation

"*50 Lessons* is a powerful reminder that greatness has its roots in faithful and devoted warriors steeped in values ingrained by the experiences of life. Without question, anyone who reads this book will be richly rewarded and sincerely blessed by the wisdom shared by one of this generation's most influential leaders."

Steve Worthy
Managing Partner
John Hancock Financial Network

"The book is a great read for all regardless of their career. The many lessons I have learned from Jack and Garry over the last 20+ years, along with the 50 lessons incorporated in this book, provide a great foundation upon which to build your life and business. They have been great topics of discussion with my daughters over dinner."

Alan Niemann
Managing Partner
The Niemann General Agency
John Hancock Financial Network

"It would only be a slight overstatement to say that everything I learned about building a record-breaking agency I learned from Garry and Jack Kinder. It's an absolute delight to devour this book and drink the wisdom direct from the sources. This book will be required reading for experienced and new agents and managers at the Barnum Financial Group, an office of MetLife. I recommend other agency directors who have **their** sights set on excellence buy this in bulk and do the same."

Paul Blanco
Managing Director
Barnum Financial Group
MetLife's Number One Office, 2004 and 2005

To order additional copies of *50 Lessons in 50 Years*,
please call 1.800.372.7110 or visit www.**KBIgroup**.com

Thank you for reading *50 Lessons in 50 Years*.
We hope it has assisted you in your quest for
personal and professional growth.

CornerStone Leadership is committed to provide new
and enlightening products to organizations worldwide.
Our mission is to fuel knowledge with practical resources
that will accelerate your team's productivity,
success and job satisfaction!

Best wishes for your continued success.

CornerStone
Leadership Institute
www.CornerStoneLeadership.com

Start a crusade in your organization –
have the courage to learn, the vision to lead,
and the passion to share.